FOR THE WOUNDED

ELEGIES FOR THE SOUL

MER MONSON

PINK POETRY

First Published in USA by Pink Poetry, LLC

In partnership with IW Press Ltd

Cover and interior artwork used with kind permission from Darcy Lee Saxton

Author photo by Justin Hackworth
Artist photo by Aline Memmott
Cover design by Iain Hill, 18 Design Ltd
Interior design by Catherine Williams, Chapter One Book Design

ISBN-13: 979-8-9938713-0-1 (Paperback)
ISBN-13: 979-8-9938713-1-8 (Hardcover)
ISBN-13: 979-8-9938713-2-5 (e-book)

Pink Poetry, LLC, Cedar Hills UT

IW Press Ltd: https://www.iliffe-wood.co.uk/

IN PRAISE OF *FOR THE WOUNDED*

In this potent collection of poems, Mer Monson is at once raw and defiant. She invites the reader to kiss the darkness, to untangle from the deceptions of a human world that is too often cloaked in pieties and self-deceptions. Approaching this poetry with open heart, one is left with a sense of rhythm—the intimate rise and fall of breath in a wounded body that is full of grace and awesomely alive.

—Thomas McConkie, author of *Atonement: Embodying the Fullness of Human Divinity*

Qarrtsiluni is an Inuit word that means sitting together in the dark, waiting for something to happen. It expresses a rich image: uncertainty, togetherness, patience but also expectancy. Mer puts words to this particular stillness of waiting, pouring a balm down each page. These are poems of spacious and unflinching compassion, insight, and invitation.

—Susan M. Hinckley, author and co-creator of *At Last She Said It*

The words on these pages wrapped me in experience, plunged me into the depths of my own humanity and kept me safe, swaddled in their poetry, while I observed that which is too chaotic and raw to look at without a guardian, a guide, an armature to hold me the way these channeled verses did. Thank you, Mer, for taking me in a glass-bottomed boat of poetry to the depths of my inner ocean and back.

—Anna Holtzman, transformational coach

When I read this manuscript, I felt as I had when first reading Rilke's Duino Elegies. Mer has captured that same depth of contemplative power—but in a voice even more resonant to me. Each poem feels like a breath taken after holding too much in for too long—tender, true, and brave. These poems do what only the truest writing can: remind us we are not alone.

—Jules Swales, writing teacher and poet

These elegies invite me to slow down, to sip loss like honeyed tea, letting each line linger before it slips inward toward the heart. Some sentences were so profound I had to speak them aloud. This is a book I'll return to whenever I need to remember the beauty in grief, to feel connected to what makes us deeply human—and to remember that sorrow can also be a doorway to the sacred.

—Laura Martin Bovard, Founder and
Creative Director, LMB Interiors

I had the great privilege of hearing Mer Monson read *For The Wounded*, but getting to read Mer's remarkable words, to linger on some extraordinary line, is an equally wonderful gift. As a professional musician I have always loved the phrase, "Where words end, music begins." In a similar fashion, Mer's poetry resonates in some deeper, truer part of myself.

—Reid Harris, Principal Viola, retired,
Atlanta Symphony Orchestra

For the Wounded is a profound meditation into being human in a world that can feel indifferent to our struggles and heartaches. I am asked to ponder how beauty, love, and suffering are not only intertwined, but essential to feeling fully alive.

—Kristy Halvorsen, Author of *Perfect Unfolding*

It is a holy thing to witness Mer's intimacy with herself and with God. She stands in the fire with unflinching grace, offering her truth like a psalm from the marrow. Her words broke something ancient in me. Tears spilled—of recognition, of reverence, of yearning. I drank them like prayer and found myself aching for more.

—Anna Scott, wisdom coach

These poetic meditations probe the awe and angst of existence. The poetry is beautiful, the honesty startling as each poem petitions and penetrates a self within self. This collection is a heart-rending journey through life and death, grief and love, fear and beauty, hopelessness and comfort, body and soul.

—Maxine Hanks, author, editor, theologian

For my siblings
Bev, Jenni, Kathy, Ron and Bub

How easy it is to see you are wholly beloved

"There is no bloom without root and darkness."

Sarah Blondin

"The call to serve God is first and last the call to be fully human."

Barbara Brown Taylor

CONTENTS

Prelude	1
For the Broken	5
For the Angels	7
For the Performer	11
For the Heart	13
For the Poet	17
For the Women Who Love Them	19
For the Disconsolate	23
For the Frightened	25
For the Faithful	29
For the Wounded	31
Gratitude	35
Connect with Mer	37
About the Author	39
About the Artist	41

PRELUDE

When my writing mentor, Jules Swales, introduced me to Rilke's *Duino Elegies*, I fell in love. I found deep permission, in his words, to stop fighting the dark – to speak stripped-down truth about my pain, fear and loss; about the transformation of my childhood faith; about living in a wounded and fragile body.

I read and re-read Rilke's laments. I wept and I wrote, playing with similar textures of language.

What emerged on the page brought me back home to my own skin, my own heart, my own broken and radiant life.

What emerged was my own redemptive response to being heartbreakingly human: be as honest as I can about it; turn toward all its mystery, ache and glory with tenderness; and let my body and soul make art.

What emerged, in the honesty of the dark, was light; a light that showed itself without pretense or strain.

During the creation of these poems, I felt their resonance with the inner-world paintings of Darcy Lee Saxton. I've loved her transformative work for many years, and I'm thrilled she has generously shared her art as an illumination of my own.

From my wounded, wild, beautiful heart to yours,

Mer

FOR THE BROKEN

If the body cries out into pitch black,
legs huddled close, face streaked with despair,
who will answer but the steady squeeze of the heart
in infinite silence? Reach up—
where is the divine face to feel with our fingers,
the wet eyes weeping, the lips of mercy whispering
into this solitary cavern of bones?

O the terrible aloneness of being a being,
never seeing what horror awaits,
submerged in a sleep of forgetting,
flung as driftwood on ever-moving water.
Drenched, each finger draws the face of God,
robes Him in promises,
suckles to fill the emptiness.

Have you not noticed? We are unlovable, scarred and unholy.
If an eternal being drips frailty into our pores,
bruises us by each other's pain from the beginning,
on whom can we fall? Where are angels,
moved in gossamer bodies by our anguish?

No angel, mother or lover crawls back to that place
before we were broken. Only the rise and fall of the belly,
sun-warmed earth, the sound of trinkets
slipping through hands that reach for a pristine God,
reach for a home the mind cannot will itself to remember.

The only kindness is to gentle this one broken heart,
to spill out her tears for a cup of quiet. Only then
can wind breathe hope through holes in the body
to the roots that were given, where hands can feel
the edge of God's face
in the bleak and humble doorway.

FOR THE ANGELS

Do you not know, dear Angel, how we long to die?
These soft shells are weary, maimed, stripped in memories
that shackle to terror. Every resting place, sifting sand.
Is it any wonder we conjure your wings at the sharp edge
of this wild and ferocious life?

How the body aches to be you,
to shed the cramped despair of love not given—
to rise up, hurt dripping through tired feet,
inclined toward each mortal's agony
without touching the flame.

Are you, dear Angel, a buried mother, father,
come to bandage your wounds
this body still carries,
drain your tears from this sorrowful chest?

In your reach for our redemption,
do you long to re-inhabit this body of cracked clay,
alit as a temporary being?—
Skin against grass and stone; vastness of stars
from a patch of dirt; truth, beating its drum
in all our shadows; contractions of light at the prison door;
loss twisting into rivers of mercy.

Would you shed your wings for this—
to see your child's face again, unblemished?
To be adored, by a blind soul,
who caresses the heart into believing it is eternal, almost?
Oh, how we stretch for love,
its force mighty and deep against this fragile body.
Come, Angel, sway us to kiss the terror,
to go soft in the pummeling.

FOR THE PERFORMER

The mind, how it gnaws. How it pummels
meaningless obsession, hour after hour,
fumbling from room to room in a house of skin.
There are no stars in the labyrinth of sinew and bone,
only restless streams of desire and more desire
winding and twisting limbs to contort
in a kaleidoscope of hunger.

And so the performer steps up, tears brushed away
for the glittery task. In zipped-up costume,
the body tumbles in feeling, twirls for love,
swoons at smiles that drop in the night before taking a bow,
suspended above forgotten depths.

Why does the spirit turn away from the breath
of emptiness, ever a stranger to that sliver of light
where no one is standing?

Too soon the body shrivels against sand and surf,
rocks and trees. In ten thousand blinks,
one solitary life on a wire
spins through the black of everything,
grasps meaning out of thin air as the ground rises up
to swallow her bones in a spray of stars.

Be still in death's whisper, Beloved.
Feel it shape your hands to cup the precious liquid
while it glistens.

FOR THE HEART

How maddening to be alive yet blind, embattled
in a split mind. To lose, too soon, a child's bright gaze,
that stretched-out wonder in a play of shadow and light.
How love breathes in a small body,
a body that is other, more real—without death in the eyes,
without grip, without calloused walls.

Death creeps closer with counted heartbeats.
Lungs and muscle clench against death's pull
as badgering of limbs ushers heartache into the quiet center,
stolen from that ledge where flight takes us.

There must be a reason not to abandon but to breathe,
to open, to wait in the dark question.

O heart, swirled in a desert of thirst and threat, how you love
and only love, never holding back sweet nourishment
as you gather stones to shield each cut.
Love is too wide, too strong for your earnest muscle.

Death knocks at the shoulders, you pump and plunge,
faithful 'til you bleed out.

Contract and the heart will wither, but to find a thin slant
of child's light— this is magic. To hold close its naked glow,
step off as sky spins, crack wide in the falling.

FOR THE POET

Each poet and theosopher reaches for why the soul
becomes flesh, yet to provoke purpose
is merely to soothe when to be here, embodied,
is already too much.

In ancient layers of pious superstition,
there is no prayer to save a body from sinking into dirt,
no hymn to keep the heart from shattering.

Happiness, that unmanageable fairy, distracts for a moment,
but the cry of grief always awaits.
How unreasonable the affliction—to lose a thousand times,
to yearn for a way to keep from disappearing,
to be beaten and sore in tainted love.

Oh earth, rough and unkind,
how you seduce into full immersion!
To push against is nothing but ache and groan,
the body but a stream, full and evanescent,
drawing breath out of darkness
until the thought of her is carried home.

It is not the depths that brought you here, Beloved,
but the simple,
though human eyes cannot still enough to see its face.
It is unsayable, yet let the spirit grasp for words
to wrap around this frail wonder,
to thin the doorway between madness and surrender,
between silence and the unstoppable river of things, if only
for the sake of a raw and luminous poem.

FOR THE WOMEN WHO LOVE THEM

How soon a mother knows a son is not her own;
Even bathed in the womb, an alien to the inner ocean of her,
until she contracts, brings him forth in harsh light
to hold him close, sing a golden melody, whisper a dream
to save him from the sinister. It is only the sound
of a gentle short forgetting.

Beneath her kisses, a storm swirls
in the valley of his hips, up through forest under his ribs,
rising flames from the ancient battlefield
of fathers grown wild.

Boy to man, caught between volcanic roots
and the world's taunt to cage each tenderness,
his mighty heart retreats. What can be done,
terror biting at the heels, to soothe this molten inner space?
The prolonged ache of a woman, the wrench of tears—
ever her body, whole on the altar, cannot save.
Each embrace, a respite, but the years are long;
his heart must be carried up the mountain alone.

Woman, if you must, reach down into the dense mystery
of your lover. Lie with him while violence sleeps;
spill passion into this knotted labyrinth that leaves bruises
on your bones, this ravaged soil that cannot answer
the wide slow river of your longing.

As you stand at the edge of the trees,
shining your ache between tall dark towers of hurt,
do not lose the sound of rushing water.

FOR THE DISCONSOLATE

Does the earth care if the body moves daring or shy
toward its end? Love cradles each dream
beneath the human tumble, yet the soul
wants to unfurl, wants to be beautiful
as it clings for survival with a shrunken heart.

Weary for the solace of a kind hour, unable to emerge
from the soil of earthly disaster,
how few let the hidden voice speak.

To birth something new, contract through the night
into creation—this is love at its fullest stretch.
This is the moment angels weep.
Light leaks into a sea of trembling lives as a swell of hope,
a balm, a waking of intimate wishes.

O mountain in the soul,
do not shrink against the steadfast arrogance of life.
A tree, not wary about where to stand,
plunges forth green shoots every time the sun
warms her drenched desire. Rise up,
let each yearning shake alive. Pour your glory out.

Do not forget the surge in a woman's belly,
ripe and heavy with unborn fruit. Hear the cry of desire
as it squeezes through the narrow canal,
how the heroine clutches fear between her legs,
rides the devil to break free the constriction
from her tired, angry hips.

Hearts burn as she raises her offering,
this glimmering burst of love turned flesh.

FOR THE FRIGHTENED

The soul has a secret craving to be wild,
but the body turns ever away from full exposure.
Only the animal lives in exquisite emptiness
without crippling gravity of self.
How did brooding become the body's hidden name?
A foreigner in its own land, the human ties itself
in intricate patterns of superstitious string,
in the cacophony of ritual, in a knot of people and things.

Oh that the mind could fling from the nest,
submerge in the current, hibernate and howl
without turning upon itself in a torrent
of reasons, a maze of unchosen paths.

The human creature does not begin this way,
lost to a separate world.
Look in the infant's eyes, into full frontal eternity.
There is no gap, no side glance, no curling in against the light.
Too soon the mind warps in artificial costume,
acting on a stage of dead trees, scarred and brittle bodies,
mere spectators of a lost and swollen heart.

Awakened only for a moment by the love-lit orgasm of birth,
it is death that comes to save. O death, most pungent gift!
Only your beautiful shock opens eyes.
Only you, dearest companion, reach down
into the body's abyss where weeping never stops
to squeeze the wild heart, hungry to come alive
in a fierce rush of forgetting.

FOR THE FAITHFUL

Each traveler is ever alone, yet the earth of the body knows
how to speak to God. Each birthright prayer,
uttered or silent, wakes the forest,
locks eyes with the hawk,
takes refuge in the rock's deep cave.

Does each asking hold back the precious catastrophe?
Not an inch, yet supplication cleanses desire
as it fills the human cathedral,
stained glass windows spilling water and light.

Earth does not care how long each sojourner dwells,
every heartbeat a revelation. Yet some, bright and stunning,
leave not knowing that to be alive is the supernal thing—
to suspend bliss, awake and thumping, to clutch pain's gravity
as it wraps around the spine, to feel each change of sky
in every tender pore. Only the aged see beneath skin
to a vast desert blooming.
Only the aged stoke heaven within.
Only the aged know love unfeigned asks not for an answer.

The end of suffering comes with its wide
and welcoming doorway, but do not provoke.
Hold each shard of tinted glass, Beloved,
as the body flails and longing takes flight.

FOR THE WOUNDED

In the moment when all that festers has gone quiet,
and the soul rests on a high ledge to survey the devastation,
it will appear—how the body shaped angst
into a bright painting of praise.
Then will the heart cry out in adoration
to each hard pull of misery's hand
that begged the body to wake.

Nothing moves the soul like thick, black pain,
yet oh, how the mind refuses these fertile arms.
How far the spirit must travel—through the warfare
of a thousand reasons, through intoxication,
through shallow salve of holy ritual, before she arrives,
at last, in the lush green valley of sorrow,
where the body does not abandon itself for the sake of heaven
but thrashes and moans in star-burning transfiguration
of pain's ecstasy unwrapped all the way to its center.

Oh heart, do not turn from this dark threshold,
where love's unyielding demand is laid bare,
where joy does not abandon each stream of melancholy
but wholly wraps around it, drinks full and deep as trampled,
blood-stained agony turns to wine.

What beauty each sadness blooms.
Come, Beloved, let grief ascend her throne.
Let all weeping illuminate your face
as you lie skin to skin with the tender thrashing.

GRATITUDE

Rainer Maria Rilke, for giving me access to the deepest recesses of my heart.

Jules Swales for putting me on the page with Rilke, for fanning the flame of my voice to grow strong and bright.

Darcy Lee Saxton, for your warm generosity in contributing to this project, for waking up that space in me where true art comes from.

Michael Neill, for breaking me open to the light within.

Anna Holtzman, for enticing my body and mind into the way of tenderness.

My fellow Method writers, for showing me my words can glow.

Maria Iliffe-Wood, my publishing partner, for holding my hand through this adventure with wisdom, competence and love.

Iain Hill and Catherine Williams, for transforming my vision onto the page.

My Sangha Sisters, for fueling the fire of my inner knowing.

Cole, Cam and Kai, for giving me a thousand ways to feel alive.

Steve, my beloved, for adoring me with abandon, for calling me a writer.

CONNECT WITH MER

If these poems speak to your heart and soul, a brief review is most welcome on your reading platform of choice.

If you'd like to engage with Mer, read more of her work, or follow her future writing adventures, visit:

https://mermonson.com
https://mermonson.substack.com/

ABOUT THE AUTHOR

Mer Monson fell in love with writing during a cancer adventure in 2015, and she has studied Method Writing since 2019. She is the author of *Reality Bathed in Hope* and a featured author in *Stories from the Muses*. Her essays and poems have been published in *Shark Reef*, *Adanna*, *Exponent II Magazine*, *Exponent II Blog*, *Say More* and *Method Writers Speak*. She lives with her husband and three sons in the Rocky Mountains of Cedar Hills, Utah.

ABOUT THE ARTIST

Darcy Lee Saxton is a visual artist whose work explores the intuitive, spiritual, and feminine forces that shape creation. She paints with layered acrylics and symbolic imagery to create pieces meant to be felt as much as seen. Originally from the Pacific Northwest, she currently lives in Southern Utah with her husband and two children. Explore more of her work at www.darcyleeart.com.

www.ingramcontent.com/pod-product-compliance
Lightning Source LLC
Jackson TN
JSHW041337250226
98530JS00003B/9
* 9 7 9 8 9 9 3 8 7 1 3 0 1 *